Mahomet

Voltaire

Translation by William F. Fleming

To His Majesty the King of Prussia.

Wilder Publications, Inc.
PO Box 10641
Blacksburg, VA 24063

ISBN 10: 1-61720-258-4
ISBN 13: 978-1-61720-258-2

First Edition

10 9 8 7 6 5 4 3 2 1

Contents

Dramatis Personæ

Mahomet.
Zopir, Sheik of Mecca.
Omar, General and second in command to Mahomet.
Seid, Slave to Mahomet.
Palmira, Slave to Mahomet.
Phanor, Senator of Mecca.
Company of Meccans.
Company of Mussulmans.

This powerful work was read by Voltaire to Frederick of Prussia in 1740, to the king's great delight. The following correspondence has peculiar interest. In his "Life of Voltaire" James Parton says: "The great lesson of the play is that the founders of false religions at once despise and practise upon the docile credulity of men. When I remember that this powerful exhibition of executive force triumphing over credulity and weakness was vividly stamped upon the susceptible brain of Frederick by Voltaire's impassioned declamation, at the very time he was revolving his Silesian project, I am inclined to the conjecture that it may have been the deciding influence upon the king's mind." The play was withdrawn after the fourth representation, under pressure of Church authorities who professed to see in it a "bloody satire against the Christian religion." This letter preserves the original characteristics.

To His Majesty the King of Prussia.
Rotterdam, January 20, 1742.
Sir:

I am at present, like the pilgrims of Mecca, turning their eyes perpetually towards that city after leaving it, as I do mine towards the court of Prussia. My heart, deeply penetrated with the sense of your majesty's goodness, knows no grief but that which arises from my incapacity of being always with you. I have taken the liberty to send your majesty a fresh copy of "Mahomet," the sketch of which you have seen some time ago. This is a tribute which I pay to the lover of arts, the sensible critic, and above all, to the philosopher much more than to the sovereign. Your majesty knows by what motive I was inspired in the composition of that work. The love of mankind, and the hatred of fanaticism, two virtues that adorn your throne, guided my pen: I have ever been of opinion, that tragedy should correct, as well as move the heart. Of what consequence or importance to mankind are the passions or misfortunes of any of the heroes of antiquity, if they do not convey some instruction to us? It is universally acknowledged, that the comedy of "Tartuffe," a piece hitherto unequalled, did a great deal of good in the world, by showing hypocrisy in its proper light; and why therefore should we not endeavor in a tragedy to expose that species of imposture which sets to work the hypocrisy of some, and the madness of others? Why may we not go back to the histories of those ancient ruffians, the illustrious founders of superstition and fanaticism, who first carried the sword to the altar to sacrifice all those who refused to embrace their doctrines?

They who tell us that these days of wickedness are past, that we shall never see any more Barcochebas, Mahomets, Johns of Leyden, etc., and that the flames of religious war are totally extinguished, in my opinion, pay too high a compliment to human nature. The same poison still subsists, though it does not appear so openly—some symptoms of this plague break out from time to time—enough to infect the earth: have not we in our own age seen the prophets of Cévennes killing in the name of God those of their sect, who were not sufficiently pliant to their purposes?

The action I have described is terrible; I do not know whether horror was ever carried farther on any stage. A young man born with virtuous inclinations, seduced by fanaticism, assassinates an old man who loves him; and whilst he imagines he is serving God, is, without knowing it, guilty of parricide: the murder is committed by the order of an impostor, who promises him a reward, which proves to be incest. This, I acknowledge, is full of horror; but your majesty is thoroughly sensible, that tragedy should not consist merely of love, jealousy, and marriage: even our histories abound in actions much more horrible than that which I have invented. Seid does not know that the person whom he assassinates is his father, and when he has committed the crime, feels the deepest remorse for it; but Mézeray tells us, that at Milan a father killed his son with his own hand on account of religion, and was not in the least sorry for it. The story of the two brothers Diaz is well known; one of them was at Rome and the other in Germany, in the beginning of the commotions raised by Luther: Bartholomew Diaz, hearing that his brother embraced the opinion of Luther at Frankfort, left Rome on purpose to assassinate him, and accordingly did so. Herrera, a Spanish author, tells us, that Bartholomew Diaz ran a great hazard in doing this, but nothing intimidates a man of honor guided by honesty. Herrera, we see, brought up in that holy religion which is an enemy to cruelty, a religion which teaches long-suffering and not revenge, was persuaded that honesty might make a man an assassin and a parricide: ought we not to rise up on all sides against such infernal maxims? These put the poniard into the hand of that monster who deprived France of Henry the Great: these placed the picture of James Clement on the altar, and his name amongst the saints: these took away the life of William, prince of Orange, founder of the liberty and prosperity of his country. Salcede shot at and wounded him in the forehead with a pistol; and Strada tells us, that Salcede would not dare to undertake that enterprise till he had purified his soul by confession at the feet of a Dominican, and fortified it by the holy sacrament. Herrera has something more horrible, and more ridiculous concerning it. "He stood firm," says he, "after the example of our Saviour, Jesus Christ, and His saints." Balthasar Girard, who afterwards took away the life of that great man, behaved in the same manner as Salcede.

I have remarked, that all those who voluntarily committed such crimes were young men like Seid. Balthasar Girard was about twenty years old, and the four Spaniards who had bound themselves by oath with him to kill the prince, were of the same age. The monster who killed Henry III., was but four-and-twenty, and Poltrot, who assassinated the great Duke of Guise only twenty-five: this is the age of seduction and madness. In England I was once a witness to how far the power of fanaticism could work on a weak and youthful imagination: a boy of sixteen, whose name was Shepherd, engaged to assassinate King George I., your majesty's grandfather by the mother's side. What could prompt him to such madness? the only reason to be assigned was, that Shepherd was not of the same religion with the king. They took pity on his youth, offered him his pardon, and for a long time endeavored to bring him to repentance; but he always persisted in saying, it was better to obey God than man; and if they let him go, the first use he made of his liberty should be to kill the king: so that they were obliged at last to execute him as a monster, whom they despaired of bringing to any sense of reason.

I will venture to affirm that all who have seen anything of mankind must have remarked how easily nature is sometimes sacrificed to superstition: how many fathers have detested and disinherited their children! how many brothers have persecuted brothers on this destructive principle! I have myself seen instances of it in more than one family.

If superstition does not always signalize itself in those glaring crimes which history transmits to us, in society it does every day all the mischief it possibly can: disunites friends, separates kindred and relations, destroys the wise and worthy by the hands of fools and enthusiasts: it does not indeed every day poison a Socrates, but it banishes Descartes from a city which ought to be the asylum of liberty, and gives Jurieu, who acted the part of a prophet, credit enough to impoverish the wise philosopher Bayle: it banished the successor of the great Leibnitz, and deprives a noble assembly of young men that crowded to his lectures, of pleasure and improvement: and to re-establish him heaven must raise up amongst us a royal philosopher, that true miracle which is so rarely to be seen. In vain does human reason advance towards perfection, by means of that philosophy which of late has made so great a progress in Europe: in vain do you, most noble prince, both inspire and practise this humane philosophy: whilst in the same age wherein reason raises her throne on one side, the most absurd fanaticism adorns her altars on the other.

It may perhaps be objected to me, that, out of my too abundant zeal, I have made Mahomet in this tragedy guilty of a crime which in reality he was not capable of committing. The count de Boulainvilliers, some time since, wrote the life of this prophet, whom he endeavored to represent as a great man, appointed by Providence to punish the Christian world, and change the face of at least one-half of the globe. Mr. Sale likewise, who has given us an excellent translation of the Koran into English, would persuade us to look upon Mahomet as a Numa or a Theseus. I will readily acknowledge, that we ought to respect him, if born a legitimate prince, or called to government by the voice of the people, he had instituted useful and peaceful laws like Numa, or like Theseus defended his countrymen: but for a driver of camels to stir up a faction in his village; to associate himself with a set of wretched Koreish, and persuade them that he had an interview with the angel Gabriel; to boast that he was carried up to heaven, and there received part of that unintelligible book which contradicts common sense in every page; that in order to procure respect for this ridiculous performance he should carry fire and sword into his country, murder fathers, and ravish their daughters, and after all give those whom he conquered the choice of his religion or death; this is surely what no man will pretend to vindicate, unless he was born a Turk, and superstition had totally extinguished in him the light of nature.

Mahomet, I know, did not actually commit that particular crime which is the subject of this tragedy: history only informs us, that he took away the wife of Seid, one of his followers, and persecuted Abusophan, whom I call Zopir; but what is not that man capable of, who, in the name of God, makes war against his country? It was not my design merely to represent a real fact, but real manners and characters, to make men think as they naturally must in their circumstances; but above all it was my intention to show the horrid schemes which villainy can invent, and fanaticism put in practice. Mahomet is here no more than Tartuffe in arms.

Upon the whole I shall think myself amply rewarded for my labor, if any one of those weak mortals, who are ever ready to receive the impressions of a madness foreign to their nature, should learn from this piece to guard themselves against such fatal delusions; if, after being shocked at the dreadful consequences of Seid's obedience, he should say to himself, why must I blindly follow the blind who cry out to me, hate, persecute all who are rash enough not to be of the same opinion with ourselves, even in things and matters we do not understand? what infinite service would it be to mankind to eradicate such false sentiments! A spirit of indulgence would make us all brothers; a spirit of persecution can create nothing but monsters. This I know is your majesty's opinion: to live with such a prince, and such a philosopher, would be my greatest happiness; my sincere attachment can only be equalled by my regret; but if other duties draw me away, they can never blot out the respect I owe to a prince, who talks and thinks like a man, who despises that specious gravity which is always a cover for meanness and ignorance: a prince who converses with freedom, because he is not afraid of being known; who is still eager to be instructed, and at the same time capable himself of instructing the most learned and the most sagacious.

I shall, whilst I have life, remain with the most profound respect, and deepest sense of gratitude, your majesty's,

Voltaire.

A Letter from M. de Voltaire to Pope Benedict XIV.

Most blessed Father—

Your holiness will pardon the liberty taken by one of the lowest of the faithful, though a zealous admirer of virtue, of submitting to the head of the true religion this performance, written in opposition to the founder of a false and barbarous sect. To whom could I with more propriety inscribe a satire on the cruelty and errors of a false prophet, than to the vicar and representative of a God of truth and mercy? Your holiness will therefore give me leave to lay at your feet both the piece and the author of it, and humbly to request your protection of the one, and your benediction upon the other; in hopes of which, with the profoundest reverence, I kiss your sacred feet.

Paris, August 17, 1745.

Voltaire.

The Answer of Pope Benedict XIV. to M. de Voltaire.

Benedictus P. P. dilecto filio salutem & Apostolicam Benedictionem.

This day sevennight I was favored with your excellent tragedy of Mahomet, which I have read with great pleasure: Cardinal Passionei has likewise presented me with your fine poem of Fontenoy. Signor Leprotti this day repeated to me your distich made on my retreat. Yesterday morning Cardinal Valenti gave me your letter of the 17th of August. Many are the obligations which you have conferred on me, for which I am greatly indebted to you, for all and every one of them; and I assure you that I have the highest esteem for your merit, which is so universally acknowledged.

The distich has been published at Rome, and objected to by one of the literati, who, in a public conversation, affirmed that there was a mistake in it with regard to the word hic, which is made short, whereas it ought to be always long. To which I replied, that it may be either long or short; Virgil having made it short in this verse,

Solus hic inflexit sensus, animumque labantem.

And long in another,

Hic finis Priami fatorum, hic exitus illum.

The answer I think was pretty full and convincing, considering that I have not looked into Virgil these fifty years. The cause, however, is properly yours; to your honor and sincerity, therefore, of which I have the highest opinion, I shall leave it to be defended against your opposers and mine, and here give you my apostolical benediction. Datum Romæ apud sanctam Mariam majorem die 19 Sept. Pontificatus nostri anno sexto.

A Letter of Thanks from M. de Voltaire to the Pope.

The features of your excellency are not better expressed on the medal you were so kind as to send me, than are the features of your mind in the letter which you honored me with: permit me to lay at your feet my sincerest acknowledgments: in points of literature, as well as in matters of more importance, your infallibility is not to be disputed: your excellency is much better versed in the Latin tongue than the Frenchman whom you condescended to correct: I am indeed astonished how you could so readily appeal to Virgil: the popes were always ranked amongst the most learned sovereigns, but amongst them I believe there never was one in whom so much learning and taste united.

Agnosco rerum dominos, gentemque togatam.

If the Frenchman who found fault with the word hic had known as much of Virgil as your excellency, he might have recollected a verse where hic is both long and short.

Hic vir hic est tibi quem promitti sæpius audis.

I cannot help considering this verse as a happy presage of the favors conferred on me by your excellency. Thus might Rome cry out when Benedict XIV. was raised to the papacy: with the utmost respect and gratitude I kiss your sacred feet, etc.

    Voltaire.

ACT I.

Scene, Mecca.

SCENE I.

Zopir, Phanor.

Zopir: Thinkest thou thy friend will ever bend the knee To this proud hypocrite; shall I fall down And worship, I who banished him from Mecca? No: punish me, just heaven, as I deserve, If e'er this hand, the friend of innocence And freedom, stoop to cherish foul rebellion, Or aid imposture to deceive mankind!

Phanor: Thy zeal is noble, and becomes the chief Of Ishmael's sacred senate, but may prove Destructive to the cause it means to serve: Thy ardor cannot check the rapid power Of Mahomet, and but provokes his vengeance: There was a time when you might safely draw The sword of justice, to defend the rights Of Mecca, and prevent the flames of war From spreading o'er the land; then Mahomet Was but a bold and factious citizen, But now he is a conqueror, and a king; Mecca's impostor at Medina shines A holy prophet; nations bend before him, And learn to worship crimes which we abhor. Even here, a band of wild enthusiasts, drunk With furious zeal, support his fond delusions, His idle tales, and fancied miracles: These spread sedition through the gaping throng, Invite his forces, and believe a God Inspires and renders him invincible. The lovers of their country think with you, But wisest counsels are not always followed; False zeal, and fear, and love of novelty Alarm the crowd; already half our city Is left unpeopled; Mecca cries aloud To thee her father, and demands a peace.

Zopir: Peace with a traitor! coward nation, what Can you expect but slavery from a tyrant! Go, bend your supple knees, and prostrate fall Before the idol whose oppressive hand Shall crush you all: for me, I hate the traitor; This heart's too deeply wounded to forgive: The savage murderer robbed me of a wife And two dear children: nor is his resentment Less fierce than mine; I forced his camp, pursued The coward to his tent, and slew his son: The torch of hatred is lit up between us, And time can never extinguish it.

Phanor: I hope It never will; yet thou shouldst hide the flame, And sacrifice thy griefs to public good: What if he lay this noble city waste, Will that avenge thee, will that serve thy cause? Thou hast lost all, son, brother, daughter, wife. Mecca alone remains to give thee comfort, Do not lose that, do not destroy thy country.

Zopir: Kingdoms are lost by cowardice alone.

Phanor: As oft perhaps by obstinate resistance.

Zopir: Then let us perish, if it be our fate.

Phanor: When thou art almost in the harbor, thus To brave the storm is false and fatal courage: Kind heaven, thou seest, points out to thee the means To soften this proud tyrant; fair Palmira, Thy beautous captive, brought up in the camp Of this destructive conqueror, was sent By gracious heaven, the messenger of peace, Thy guardian angel, to appease the wrath Of Mahomet; already by his herald He has demanded her.

Zopir: And wouldst thou have me Give up so fair a prize to this barbarian? What! whilst the tyrant spreads destruction round him, Unpeoples kingdoms, and destroys mankind, Shall beauty's charms be sacrificed to bribe A madman's frenzy? I should envy him That lovely fair one more than all his glory; Not that I feel the stings of wild desire, Or, in the evening of my days, indulge, Old as I am, a shameless passion for her; But, whether objects born like her to please, Spite of ourselves, demand our tenderest pity, Or that perhaps a childless father hopes To find in her another daughter, why I know not, but for that unhappy maid Still am I anxious; be it weakness in me, Or reason's powerful voice, I cannot bear To see her in the hands of Mahomet; Would I could mould her to my wishes, form Her willing mind, and make her hate the tyrant As I do! She has sent to speak with me Here in the sacred porch—and lo! she comes: On her fair cheek the blush of modesty And candor speaks the virtues of her heart.

SCENE II.

Zopir, Palmira.

Zopir: Hail, lovely maid! the chance of cruel war Hath made thee Zopir's captive, but thou art not Amongst barbarians; all with me revere Palmira's virtues, and lament her fate, Whilst youth with innocence and beauty plead Thy cause; whatever thou askest in Zopir's power, Thou shalt not ask in vain: my life declines Towards its period, and if my last hours Can give Palmira joy, I shall esteem them The best, the happiest I have ever known.

Palmira: These two months past, my lord, your prisoner here, Scarce have I felt the yoke of slavery; Your generous hand, still raised to soothe affliction, Hath wiped the tears of sorrow from my eyes, And softened all the rigor of my fate: Forgive me, if emboldened by your goodness I ask for more, and centre every hope Of future happiness on you alone; Forgive me, if to Mahomet's request I join Palmira's, and implore that freedom He hath already asked: O listen to him, And let me say, that after heaven and him I am indebted most to generous Zopir.

Zopir: Has then oppression such enticing charms That thou shouldst wish and beg to be the slave Of Mahomet, to hear the clash of arms, With him to live in deserts, and in caves, And wander o'er his ever shifting country?

Palmira: Where'er the mind with ease and pleasure dwells, There is our home, and there our native country: He formed my soul; to Mahomet I owe The kind instruction of my earlier years; Taught by the happy partners of his bed, Who still adoring and adored by him Send up their prayers to heaven for his dear safety, I lived in peace and joy! for ne'er did woe Pollute that seat of bliss till the sad hour Of my misfortune, when wide-wasting war Rushed in upon us and enslaved Palmira: Pity, my lord, a heart oppressed with grief, That sighs for objects far, far distant from her.

Zopir: I understand you, madam; you expect The tyrant's hand, and hope to share his throne.

Palmira: I honor him, my lord; my trembling soul Looks up to Mahomet with holy fear As to a god; but never did this heart E'er cherish the vain hope that he would deign To wed Palmira: No: such splendor ill Would suit my humble state.

Zopir: Whoe'er thou art, He was not born, I trust, to be thy husband, No, nor thy master; much I err, or thou Springest from a race designed by heaven to check This haughty Arab, and give laws to him Who thus assumes the majesty of kings.

Palmira: Alas! we know not what it is to boast Of birth or fortune; from our infant years Without or parents, friends, or country, doomed To slavery; here resigned to our hard fate, Strangers to all but to that God we serve, We live content in humble poverty.

Zopir: And can ye be content? and are ye strangers, Without a father, and without a home? I am a childless, poor, forlorn, old man; You might have been the comfort of my age: To form a plan of future happiness For you, had softened my own wretchedness, And made me some amends for all my wrongs: But you abhor my country and my law.

Palmira: I am not mistress of myself, and how Can I be thine? I pity thy misfortunes, And bless thee for thy goodness to Palmira; But Mahomet has been a father to me.

Zopir: A father! ye just gods! the vile impostor!

Palmira: Can he deserve that name, the holy prophet, The great ambassador of heaven, sent down To interpret its high will?

Zopir: Deluded mortals! How blind ye are, to follow this proud madman, This happy robber, whom my justice spared, And raise him from the scaffold to a throne!

Palmira: My lord, I shudder at your imprecations; Though I am bound by honor and the ties Of gratitude to love thee for thy bounties, This blasphemy against my kind protector Cancels the bond, and fills my soul with horror. O superstition, how thy savage power Deprives at once the best and tenderest hearts Of their humanity!

Zopir: Alas! Palmira, Spite of myself, I feel for thy misfortunes, Pity thy weakness, and lament thy fate.

Palmira: You will not grant me then—

Zopir: I cannot yield thee To him who has deceived thy easy heart, To a base tyrant; No: thou art a treasure Too precious to be parted with, and makest This hypocrite but more detested.

SCENE III.

Zopir, Palmira, Phanor.

Zopir: Phanor, What wouldst thou?

Phanor: At the city gate that leads To Moad's fertile plain, the valiant Omar Is just arrived.

Zopir: Indeed; the tyrant's friend, The fierce, vindictive Omar, his new convert, Who had so long opposed him, and still fought For us!

Phanor: Perhaps he yet may serve his country, Already he hath offered terms of peace; Our chiefs have parleyed with him, he demands An hostage, and I hear they've granted him The noble Seid.

Palmira: Seid? gracious heaven!

Phanor: Behold! my lord, he comes.

Zopir: Ha! Omar here! There's no retreating now, he must be heard; Palmira, you may leave us.—O ye gods Of my forefathers, you who have protected The sons of Ishmael these three thousand years, And thou, O Sun, with all those sacred lights That glitter round us, witness to my truth, Aid and support me in the glorious conflict With proud iniquity!

SCENE IV.

Zopir, Omar, Phanor, Attendants.

Zopir: At length, it seems, Omar returns, after a three years' absence, To visit that loved country which his hand So long defended, and his honest heart Has now betrayed: deserter of our gods, Deserter of our laws, how darest thou thus Approach these sacred walls to persecute And to oppress; a public robber's slave; What is thy errand? wherefore comest thou hither?

Omar: To pardon thee: by me our holy prophet, In pity to thy age, thy well-known valor, And past misfortunes, offers thee his hand: Omar is come to bring thee terms of peace.

Zopir: And shall a factious rebel offer peace Who should have sued for pardon? gracious gods! Will ye permit him to usurp your power, And suffer Mahomet to rule mankind? Dost thou not blush, vile minion as thou art, To serve a traitor? hast thou not beheld him Friendless and poor, an humble citizen, And ranking with the meanest of the throng? How little then in fortune or in fame!

Omar: Thus low and grovelling souls like thine pretend To judge of merit, whilst in fortune's scale Ye weigh the worth of men: proud, empty being, Dost thou not know that the poor worm which crawls Low on the earth, and the imperial eagle That soars to heaven, in the all-seeing eye Of their eternal Maker are the same, And shrink to nothing? men are equal all; From virtue only true distinction springs, And not from birth: there are exalted spirits Who claim respect and honor from themselves And not their ancestors: these, these, my lord, Are heaven's peculiar care, and such is he Whom I obey, and who alone deserves To be a master; all mankind like me Shall one day fall before the conqueror's feet, And future ages follow my example.

Zopir: Omar, I know thee well; thy artful hand In vain hath drawn the visionary portrait; Thou mayest deceive the multitude, but know, What Mecca worships Zopir can despise: Be honest then, and with the impartial eye Of reason look on Mahomet; behold him But as a mortal, and consider well By what base arts the vile impostor rose, A camel-driver, a poor abject slave, Who first deceived a fond, believing woman, And now supported by an idle dream Draws in the weak and credulous multitude: Condemned to exile, I chastised the rebel Too lightly, and his insolence returns With double force to punish my indulgence. He fled with Fatima from cave to cave, And suffered chains, contempt and banishment; Meantime the fury which he called divine Spread like a subtle poison through the crowd; Medina was infected: Omar then, To reason's voice attentive, would have stopped The impetuous torrent; he had courage then And virtue to attack the proud usurper, Though now he crouches to him like a slave. If thy proud master be indeed a prophet, How didst thou dare to punish him? or why, If an impostor, wilt thou dare to serve him?

Omar: I punished him because I knew him not; But now, the veil of ignorance removed, I see him as he is; behold him born To change the astonished world, and rule mankind: When I beheld him rise in awful pomp, Intrepid, eloquent, by all admired, By all adored; beheld him speak and act, Punish and pardon like a god, I lent My little aid, and joined the conqueror. Altars, thou knowest, and thrones were our reward; Once I was blind, like thee, but, thanks to heaven! My eyes are opened now; would, Zopir, thine Were open, too! let me entreat thee, change, As I have done; no longer boast thy zeal And cruel hatred, nor blaspheme our God, But fall submissive at the hero's feet Whom thou hast injured; kiss the hand that bears The angry lightning, lest it fall upon thee. Omar is now the second of mankind; A place of honor yet remains for thee, If prudent thou wilt yield, and own a master: What we have been thou knowest, and what we are: The multitude are ever weak and blind, Made for our use, born but to serve the great, But to admire, believe us, and obey: Reign then with us, partake the feast of grandeur, No longer deign to imitate the crowd, But henceforth make them tremble.

Zopir: Tremble thou, And Mahomet, with all thy hateful train: Thinkest thou that Mecca's faithful chief will fall At an impostor's feet, and crown a rebel? I am no stranger to his specious worth; His courage and his conduct have my praise; Were he but virtuous I like thee should love him; But as he is I hate the tyrant: hence, Nor talk to me of his deceitful mercy, His clemency and goodness; all his aim Is cruelty and vengeance: with this hand I slew his darling son; I banished him: My hatred is inflexible, and so Is Mahomet's resentment: if he e'er Re-enters Mecca, he must cut his way Through Zopir's blood, for he is deeply stained With crimes that justice never can forgive.

Omar: To show thee Mahomet is merciful, That he can pardon though thou canst not, here I offer thee the third of all our spoils Which we have taken from tributary kings; Name your conditions, and the terms of peace; Set your own terms on fair Palmira; take Our treasures, and be happy.

Zopir: Thinkest thou Zopir Will basely sell his honor and his country, Will blast his name with infamy for wealth, The foul reward of guilt, or that Palmira Will ever own a tyrant for her master? She is too virtuous e'er to be the slave Of Mahomet, nor will I suffer her To fall a sacrifice to base impostors Who would subvert the laws, and undermine The safety and the virtue of mankind.

Omar: Implacably severe; thou talkest to Omar As if he were a criminal, and thou His judge; but henceforth I would have thee act A better part, and treat me as a friend, As the ambassador of Mahomet, A conqueror and a king.

Zopir: A king! who made, Who crowned him?

Omar: Victory: respect his glory, And tremble at his power: amidst his conquests The hero offers peace; our swords are still Unsheathed, and woe to this rebellious city If she submits not: think what blood must flow, The blood of half our fellow-citizens; Consider, Zopir, Mahomet is here, And even now requests to speak with thee.

Zopir: Ha! Mahomet!

Omar: Yes, he conjures thee.

Zopir: Traitor! Were I the sole despotic ruler here He should be answered soon—by chastisement.

Omar: I pity, Zopir, thy pretended virtue; But since the senate insolently claim Divided empire with thee, to the senate Let us begone; Omar will meet thee there.

Zopir: I'll follow thee: we then shall see who best Can plead his cause: I will defend my gods, My country, and her laws; thy impious voice Shall bellow for thy vengeful deity, Thy persecuting god, and his false prophet. [Turning to Phanor.] Haste, Phanor, and with me repulse the traitor; Who spares a villain is a villain:—come, Let us, my friend, unite to crush his pride, Subvert his wily purposes, destroy him, Or perish in the attempt: If Mecca listens To Zopir's councils, I shall free my country From a proud tyrant's power, and save mankind.

ACT II

SCENE I.

Seid, Palmira.

Palmira: Welcome, my Seid, do I see thee here Once more in safety? what propitious god Conducted thee? at length Palmira's woes Shall have an end, and we may yet be happy.

Seid: Thou sweetest charmer, balm of every woe, Dear object of my wishes and my tears, O since that day of blood when flushed with conquest The fierce barbarian snatched thee from my arms, When midst a heap of slaughtered friends I lay Expiring on the ground, and called on death, But called in vain, to end my hated being, What have I suffered for my dear Palmira! How have I cursed the tardy hours that long Withheld my vengeance! my distracted soul's Impatience thirsted for the bloody field, That with these hands I might lay waste this seat Of slavery, where Palmira mourned so long In sad captivity; but thanks to heaven! Our holy prophet, whose deep purposes Are far beyond the ken of human wisdom, Hath hither sent his chosen servant Omar; I flew to meet him, they required a hostage; I gave my faith, and they received it; firm In my resolve to live or die for thee.

Palmira: Seid, the very moment ere thou camest To calm my fears, and save me from despair, Was I entreating the proud ravisher; Thou knowest, I cried, the only good on earth I prized is left behind, restore it to me: Then clasped his knees, fell at the tyrant's feet, And bathed them with my tears, but all in vain: How his unkind refusal shocked my soul! My eyes grew dim, and motionless I stood As one deprived of life; no succor nigh, No ray of hope was left, when Seid came To ease my troubled heart, and bring me comfort.

Seid: Who could behold unmoved Palmira's woes?

Palmira: The cruel Zopir; not insensible He seemed to my misfortunes, yet at last Unkindly told me, I must never hope To leave these walls, for naught should tear me from him.

Seid: 'Tis false; for Mahomet, my royal master, With the victorious Omar, and forgive me, If to these noble friends I proudly add The name of Seid, these shall set thee free, Dry up thy tears, and make Palmira happy: The God of Mahomet, our great protector, That God whose sacred standard I have borne; He who destroyed Medina's haughty ramparts Shall lay rebellious Mecca at our feet; Omar is here, and the glad people look With eyes of friendship on him; in the name Of Mahomet he comes, and meditates Some noble purpose.

Palmira: Mahomet indeed Might free us, and unite two hearts long since Devoted to his cause; but he, alas! Is far removed, and we abandoned captives.

SCENE II.

palmira, seid, omar.

Omar: Despair not; heaven perhaps may yet reward you, For Mahomet and liberty are nigh.

Seid: Is he then come?

Palmira: Our friend and father?

Omar: Yes. I met the council, and by Mahomet Inspired, addressed them thus: "Within these walls, Even here," I cried, "the favorite of heaven, Our holy prophet, first drew breath; the great, The mighty conqueror, the support of kings; And will ye not permit him but to rank As friend and fellow-citizen? he comes not To ruin or enslave, but to protect, To teach you and to save, to fix his power, And hold dominion o'er the conquered heart." I spoke; the hoary sages smiled applause, And all inclined to favor us; but Zopir, Still resolute and still inflexible, Declared, the people should be called together, And give their general voice: the people met, Again I spoke, addressed the citizens, Exhorted, threatened, practised every art To win their favor, and at length prevailed; The gates are opened to great Mahomet, Who after fifteen years of cruel exile Returns to bless once more his native land; With him the gallant Ali, brave Hercides, And Ammon the invincible, besides A numerous train of chosen followers: The people throng around him; some with looks Of hatred, some with smiles of cordial love; Some bless the hero, and some curse the tyrant: Some threaten and blaspheme, whilst others fall Beneath his feet, embrace and worship him; Meantime the names of God, of peace, and freedom, Are echoed through the all-believing crowd; Whilst Zopir's dying party bellows forth In idle threats its impotent revenge: Amidst their cries, unruffled and serene, In triumph walks the god-like Mahomet, Bearing the olive in his hand; already Peace is proclaimed, and see! the conqueror comes.

SCENE III.

Mahomet, Omar, Hercides, Seid, Palmira, Attendants.

Mahomet: My friends, and fellow-laborers, valiant Ali, Morad, and Ammon, and Hercides, hence To your great work, and in my name instruct The people, lead them to the paths of truth, Promise and threaten; let my God alone Be worshipped, and let those who will not love Be taught to fear him.—Seid, art thou here?

Seid: My ever-honored father, and my king, Led by that power divine who guided thee To Mecca's walls, preventing your commands I came, prepared to live or die with thee.

Mahomet: You should have waited for my orders; he Who goes beyond his duty knows it not; I am heaven's minister, and thou art mine; Learn then of me to serve and to obey.

Palmira: Forgive, my lord, a youth's impatient ardor: Brought up together from our infant years, The same our fortunes, and our thoughts the same: Alas! my life has been a life of sorrow; Long have I languished in captivity, Far from my friends, from Seid, and from thee; And now at last, when I beheld a ray Of comfort shining on me, thy unkindness Blasts my fair hopes, and darkens all the scene.

Mahomet: Palmira, 'tis enough: I know thy virtues; Let naught disturb thee: spite of all my cares, Glory, and empire, and the weight of war, I will remember thee; Palmira still Lives in my heart, and shares it with mankind: Seid shall join our troops; thou, gentle maid, Mayest serve thy God in peace: fear naught but Zopir.

SCENE IV.

Mahomet, Omar.

Mahomet: Brave Omar, stay, for in thy faithful bosom Will I repose the secrets of my soul: The lingering progress of a doubtful siege May stop our rapid course; we must not give These weak deluded mortals too much time To pry into our actions; prejudice Rules o'er the vulgar with despotic sway. Thou knowest there is a tale which I have spread And they believe, that universal empire Awaits the prophet, who to Mecca's walls Shall lead his conquering bands, and bring her peace. 'Tis mine to mark the errors of mankind, And to avail me of them; but whilst thus I try each art to soothe this fickle people, What thinks my friend of Seid and Palmira?

Omar: I think most nobly of them, that amidst Those few staunch followers who own no God, No faith but thine, who love thee as their father, Their friend, and benefactor, none obey Or serve thee with an humbler, better mind; They are most faithful.

Mahomet: Omar, thou art deceived; They are my worst of foes, they love each other.

Omar: And can you blame their tenderness?

Mahomet: My friend, I'll tell thee all my weakness.

Omar: How, my lord!

Mahomet: Thou knowest the reigning passion of my soul; Whilst proud ambition and the cares of empire Weighed heavy on me, Mahomet's hard life Has been a conflict with opposing Nature, Whom I have vanquished by austerity, And self-denial; have banished from me That baleful poison which unnerves mankind, Which only serves to fire them into madness, And brutal follies; on the burning sand Or desert rocks I brave the inclement sky, And bear the seasons' rough vicissitude: Love is my only solace, the dear object Of all my toils, the idol I adore, The god of Mahomet, the powerful rival Of my ambition: know, midst all my queens, Palmira reigns sole mistress of my heart: Think then what pangs of jealousy thy friend Must feel when she expressed her fatal passion For Seid.

Omar: But thou art revenged.

Mahomet: Judge thou If soon I ought not to take vengeance on them: That thou mayest hate my rival more, I'll tell thee Who Seid and Palmira are—the children Of him whom I abhor, my deadliest foe.

Omar: Ha! Zopir!

Mahomet: Is their father: fifteen years Are past since brave Hercides to my care Gave up their infant years; they know not yet Or who or what they are; I brought them up Together; I indulged their lawless passion, And added fuel to the guilty flame. Methinks it is as if the hand of heaven Had meant in them to centre every crime. But I must—Ha! their father comes this way, His eyes are full of bitterness and wrath Against me—now be vigilant, my Omar, Hercides must be careful to possess This most important pass; return, and tell me Whether 'tis most expedient to declare Against him, or retreat: away.

SCENE V.

Zopir, Mahomet.

Zopir: Hard fate! Unhappy Zopir! thus compelled to meet My worst of foes, the foe of all mankind!

Mahomet: Since 'tis the will of heaven that Mahomet And Zopir should at length unite, approach Without a blush, and fearless tell thy tale.

Zopir: I blush for thee alone, whose baneful arts Have drawn thy country to the brink of ruin; Who in the bosom of fair peace wouldst wage Intestine war, loosen the sacred bonds Of friendship, and destroy our happiness; Beneath the veil of proffered terms thou meanest But to betray, whilst discord stalks before thee: Thou vile assemblage of hypocrisy And insolence, abhorred tyrant! thus Do the chosen ministers of heaven dispense Its sacred blessings, and announce their God?

Mahomet: Wert thou not Zopir, I would answer thee As thou deservest, in thunder, by the voice Of that offended Being thou deridest: Armed with the hallowed Koran I would teach thee To tremble and obey in humble silence: And with the subject world to kneel before me; But I will talk to thee without disguise, As man to man should speak, and friend to friend: I have ambition, Zopir; where's the man Who has it not? but never citizen, Or chief, or priest, or king projected aught So noble as the plan of Mahomet; In acts or arms hath every nation shone Superior in its turn; Arabia now Steps forth; that generous people, long unknown And unrespected, saw her glories sunk, Her honors lost; but, lo! the hour is come When she shall rise to victory and renown; The world lies desolate from pole to pole; India's slaves, and bleeding Persia mourns Her slaughtered sons; whilst Egypt hangs the head Dejected; from the walls of Constantine Splendor is fled; the Roman Empire torn By discord, sees its scattered members spread On every side inglorious;—let us raise Arabia on the ruins of mankind: The blind and tottering universe demands Another worship, and another God. Crete had her Minos, Egypt her Osiris, To Asia Zoroaster gave his laws, And Numa was in Italy adored: O'er savage nations where nor monarchs ruled Nor manners softened, nor religion taught, Hath many a sage his fruitless maxims spread; Beneath a nobler yoke I mean to bend The prostrate world, and change their feeble laws, Abolish their false worship, pull down Their powerless gods, and on my purer faith Found universal empire: say not, Zopir, That Mahomet betrays his country, no: I mean but to destroy its weak supports, And, banishing idolatry, unite it Beneath one king, one prophet, and one God; I shall subdue it but to make it glorious.

Zopir: Is this thy purpose then, and darest thou thus Avow it? canst thou change the hearts of men, And make them think like thee? are war and slaughter The harbingers of wisdom and of peace; Can he who ravages instruct mankind? If in the night of ignorance and error We long have wandered, must thy dreadful torch Enlighten us? What right hast thou to empire?

Mahomet: That right which firm, exalted spirits claim O'er vulgar minds.

Zopir: Thus every bold impostor May forge new fetters, and enslave mankind: He has a right, it seems, to cheat the world If he can do it with an air of grandeur.

Mahomet: I know your people well; I know they want A leader; my religion, true or false, Is needful to them: what have all your gods And all your idols done? what laurels grow Beneath their altars? your low, grovelling sect Debases man, unnerves his active soul, And makes it heavy, phlegmatic, and mean; Whilst mine exalts it, gives it strength and courage: My law forms heroes.

Zopir: Rather call them robbers: Away; nor bring thy hateful lessons here; Go to the school of tyrants, boast thy frauds To lost Medina, where thou reignest supreme, Where blinded bigots bend beneath thy power, And thou beholdest thy equals at thy feet.

Mahomet: My equals! Mahomet has none; long since I passed them all; Medina is my own, And Mecca trembles at me; if thou holdest Thy safety dear, receive the peace I offer.

Zopir: Thou talkest of peace, but 'tis not in thy heart; I'm not to be deceived.

Mahomet: I would not have thee; The weak deceive, the powerful command: To-morrow I shall force thee to submit; To-day, observe, I would have been thy friend.

Zopir: Can we be friends? can Mahomet and Zopir E'er be united? say, what god shall work A miracle like that?

Mahomet: I'll tell thee one, A powerful God, one that is always heard, By me he speaks to thee.

Zopir: Who is it? name him.

Mahomet: Interest, thy own dear interest.

Zopir: Sooner heaven And hell shall be united; interest May be the god of Mahomet, but mine Is—justice: what shall join them to each other? Where is the cement that must bind our friendship? Is it that son I slew, or the warm blood Of Zopir's house which thou has shed?

Mahomet: It is Thy blood, thy son's—for now I will unveil A secret to thee, known to none but me: Thou weepest thy children dead; they both are—living.

Zopir: What sayest thou? living? unexpected bliss! My children living?

Mahomet: Yes; and both—my prisoners.

Zopir: My children slaves to thee? impossible!

Mahomet: My bounty nourished them.

Zopir: And couldst thou spare A child of Zopir's?

Mahomet: For their father's faults I would not punish them.

Zopir: But tell me, say, For what are they reserved?

Mahomet: Their life or death Depend on me: speak but the word, and thou Art master of their fate.

Zopir: O name the price And thou shalt have it; must I give my blood, Or must I bear their chains, and be the slave Of Mahomet?

Mahomet: I ask not either of thee: Lend me thy aid but to subdue the world; Surrender Mecca to me, and give up Your temple, bid the astonished people read My sacred Koran; be thou my vassal, And fall before me, then will I restore Thy son, perhaps hereafter may reward thee With honors, and contract a closer tie With Zopir.

Zopir: Mahomet, thou seest in me A tender father: after fifteen years Of cruel absence, to behold my children, To die in their embraces, were the first And fairest blessings that my soul could wish for; But if to thee I must betray my country, Or sacrifice my children, know, proud tyrant, The choice is made already—fare thee well.

Mahomet: Inexorable dotard! but henceforth I will be more implacable, more cruel Even than thyself.

SCENE VI.

Mahomet, Omar.

Omar: And so indeed thou must be, Or all is lost: already I have bought Their secret counsels: Mahomet, to-morrow The truce expires, and Zopir reassumes His power; thy life's in danger: half the senate Are leagued against thee: those who dare not fight May hire the dark assassin to destroy thee; May screen their guilt beneath the mask of justice, And call the murder legal punishment.

Mahomet: First they shall feel my vengeance: persecution, Thou knowest, has ever been my best support. Zopir must die.

Omar: 'Tis well resolved: his fate Will teach the rest obedience: lose no time.

Mahomet: Yet, spite of my resentment, I must hide The murderous hand that deals the blow, to 'scape Suspicion's watchful eye, and not incense The multitude.

Omar: They are not worth our care.

Mahomet: And yet they must be pleased: I want an arm That will strike boldly.

Omar: Seid is the man; I'll answer for him.

Mahomet: Seid?

Omar: Ay: the best, The fittest instrument to serve our purpose: As Zopir's hostage he may find occasion To speak with him, and soon avenge his master. Thy other favorites are too wise, too prudent For such a dangerous enterprise; old age Takes off the bandage of credulity From mortal eyes; but the young, simple heart, The willing slave to its own fond opinions, And void of guile, will act as we direct it: Youth is the proper period for delusion. Seid, thou knowest, is superstitious, bold, And violent, but easy to be led; Like a tame lion, to his keeper's voice Obedient.

Mahomet: What! the brother of Palmira?

Omar: Ay; Seid, the fierce son of thy proud foe, The incestuous rival of great Mahomet, His master's rival.

Mahomet: I detest him, Omar, Abhor his very name; my murdered son Cries out for vengeance on him; but thou knowest The object of my love, and whence she sprung: Thou seest I am oppressed on every side; I would have altars, victims, and a throne; I would have Zopir's blood, and Seid's too: I must consult my interest, my revenge, My honor, and my love, that fatal passion, Which, spite of my resentment, holds this heart In shameful chains: I must consult religion, All powerful motive, and necessity That throws a veil o'er every crime: away.

ACT III.

SCENE I.

Seid, Palmira.

Palmira: O Seid, keep me not in dread suspense, What is this secret sacrifice? what blood Hath heaven demanded?

Seid: The eternal power Deigns to accept my service, calls on me To execute its purposes divine; To him this heart's devoted, and for him This arm shall rise in vengeance; I am bound To Omar and to Mahomet, have sworn To perish in the glorious cause of heaven: My next and dearest care shall be Palmira.

Palmira: Why was not I a witness to thy oath? Had I been with thee, I had been less wretched; But doubts distract me: Omar talks of treason, Of blood that soon must flow; the senate's rage, And Zopir's dark intrigues: the flames of war Once more are kindled, and the sword is drawn Heaven only knows when to be sheathed again: So says our prophet, he who cannot lie, Cannot deceive us: O I fear for Seid, Fear all from Zopir.

Seid: Can he have a heart So base and so perfidious? but this morning, When as a hostage I appeared before him, I thought him noble, generous, and humane; Some power invincible in secret worked, And won me to him; whether the respect Due to his name, or specious form external Concealed the blackness of his heart I know not; Whether thy presence filled my raptured soul With joy that drove out every painful sense, And would not let me think of aught but thee: Whate'er the cause, methought I was most happy When nearest him: that he should thus seduce My easy heart makes me detest him more; And yet how hard it is to look on those With eyes of hatred whom we wish to love!

Palmira: By every bond hath heaven united us, And Seid and Palmira are the same: Were I not bound to thee, and to that faith Which Mahomet inspires, I too had pleaded The cause of Zopir; but religion, love, And nature, all forbid it.

Seid: Think no more Of vain remorse, but listen to the voice Of heaven, the God we serve will be propitious: Our holy prophet who protects his children Will bless our faithful love: for thy dear sake I hazard all. Farewell.

SCENE II.

Palmira: [Alone.] Some dark presage Of future misery hangs o'er me still: That love which made my happiness, this day, So often wished for, is a day of horror: What is this dreadful oath, this solemn compact Which Seid talks of? I've a thousand fears Upon me when I think of Zopir: oft As I invoke great Mahomet, I feel A secret dread, and tremble as I worship: O save me, heaven! fearful I obey, And blind I follow: O direct my steps Aright, and deign to wash my tears away!

SCENE III.

mahomet, palmira.

Palmira: Propitious heaven hath heard my prayers; he comes, The prophet comes. O gracious Mahomet, My Seid—

Mahomet: What of him? thou seemest disturbed; What should Palmira fear when I am with her!

Palmira: Have I not cause when Mahomet himself Seems touched with grief?

Mahomet: Perhaps it is for thee: Darest thou, imprudent maid, avow a passion Ere I approved it: is the heart I formed Turned rebel to its master, to my laws Unfaithful? O ingratitude!

Palmira: My lord, Behold me at your feet, and pity me: Didst thou not once propitious smile upon us, And give thy sanction to our growing love? Thou knowest the virtuous passion that unites us Is but a chain that binds us more to thee.

Mahomet: The bonds that folly and imprudence knit Are dangerous; guilt doth sometimes follow close The steps of innocence: our hearts deceive us, And love, with all his store of dear delights, May cost us tears, and dip his shafts in blood.

Palmira: Nor would I murmur if it flowed for Seid.

Mahomet: Are you indeed so fond?

Palmira: E'er since the day When good Hercides to thy sacred power Consigned us both, unconquerable instinct, Still growing with our years, united us In tender friendship; 'twas the work of heaven That guides our every action, and o'errules The fate of mortals; so thy doctrines teach: God cannot change, nor gracious heaven condemn That love itself inspired: what once was right Is always so; canst thou then blame Palmira?

Mahomet: I can, and must; nay, thou wilt tremble more When I reveal the horrid secret to thee. Attend, rash maid, and let me teach thy soul What to avoid, and what to follow: listen To me alone.

Palmira: To thee alone Palmira Will listen ever, the obedient slave Of Mahomet; this heart can never lose Its veneration for thy sacred name.

Mahomet: That veneration in excess may lead To foul ingratitude.

Palmira: When I forget Thy goodness, then may Seid punish me!

Mahomet: Seid!

Palmira: O why, my lord, that cruel frown, And look severe?

Mahomet: Be not alarmed; I meant But to explore the secrets of thy heart, And try if thou wert worthy to be saved: Be confident, and rest on my protection; On your obedience will depend your fate; If ye expect a blessing at my hands, Be careful to deserve it, and whate'er The will of heaven determines touching Seid, Be thou his guide, direct him in the paths Of duty, and religion; let him keep His promise, and be worthy of Palmira.

Palmira: O he will keep it; doubt him not, my lord, I'll answer for his heart as for my own; Seid adores thee, worships Mahomet More than he loves

Palmira; thou art all To him, his friend, his father, and his king: I'll fly, and urge him to his duty.

SCENE IV.

Mahomet: [Alone.] Well: Spite of myself I must, it seems, be made A confidant; the simple girl betrayed Her guilty flame, and innocently plunged The dagger in my heart: unhappy race! Father and children, all my foes, all doomed To make me wretched! but ye soon shall prove That dreadful is my hatred—and my love.

SCENE V.

Mahomet, Omar.

Omar: At length the hour is come, to seize Palmira, To conquer Mecca, and to punish Zopir; His death alone can prop our feeble cause, And humble these proud citizens: brave Seid Can best avenge thee; he has free access To Zopir: yonder gloomy passage leads To his abode; there the rebellious chief His idle vows and flattering incense pours Before his fancied deities; there Seid, Full of the law divine by thee inspired, Shall sacrifice the traitor to the God Of Mahomet.

Mahomet: He shall: that youth was born For crimes of deepest dye: he shall be first My useful slave, my instrument, and then The victim of my rage; it must be so: My safety, my resentment, and my love, My holy faith, and the decrees of fate Irrevocable, all require it of me: But thinkest thou, Omar, he hath all the warmth Of wild fanaticism?

Omar: I know he has, And suits our purpose well; Palmira, too, Will urge him on; religion, love, resentment Will blind his headstrong youth, and hurry him To madness.

Mahomet: Hast thou bound him by an oath?

Omar: O yes; in all the gloomy pomp of rites Nocturnal, oaths, and altars, we have fixed His superstitious soul, placed in his hand The sacred sword, and fired him with the rage Of fierce enthusiasm—but behold him.

SCENE VI.

Mahomet, Omar, Seid.

Mahomet: Child Of heaven, decreed to execute the laws Of an offended God, now hear by me His sacred will: thou must avenge his cause.

Seid: O thou, to whom my soul devoted bends In humblest adoration, king, and prophet, Sovereign, acknowledged by the voice of heaven, O'er prostrate nations—I am wholly thine: But O enlighten my dark mind! O say, How can weak man avenge his God?

Mahomet: Oft-times Doth he make use of feeble hands like thine To punish impious mortals, and assert His power divine.

Seid: Will he, whose perfect image Is seen in Mahomet, thus condescend To honor Seid?

Mahomet: Do as he ordains; That is the highest honor man can boast, Blindly to execute his great decree: Be thankful for the choice, and strike the blow: The angel of destruction shall assist, The God of armies shall protect thee.

Seid: Speak; What tyrant must be slain? what blood must flow?

Mahomet: The murderer's blood whom Mahomet abhors, Who persecutes our faith, and spurns our God, Who slew my son; the worst of all my foes, The cruel Zopir.

Seid: Ha! must Zopir fall?

Mahomet: And dost thou pause? presumptuous youth! 'tis impious But to deliberate: far from Mahomet Be all who for themselves shall dare to judge Audacious; those who reason are not oft Prone to believe; thy part is to obey. Have I not told thee what the will of heaven Determines? if it be decreed that Mecca, Spite of her crimes and base idolatry, Shall be the promised temple, the chosen seat Of empire, where I am appointed king, And pontiff, knowest thou why our Mecca boasts These honors? knowest thou holy Abram here Was born, that here his sacred ashes rest? He who, obedient to the voice of God, Stifled the cries of nature, and gave up His darling child: the same all-powerful Being Requires of thee a sacrifice; to thee He calls for blood; and darest thou hesitate When God commands? hence, vile idolater, Unworthy Mussulman, away, and seek Another master; go, and love Palmira; But thou despisest her, and bravest the wrath Of angry heaven; away, forsake thy lord, And serve his deadliest foes.

Seid: It is the voice Of God that speaks in Mahomet:—command, And I obey.

Mahomet: Strike, then, and by the blood Of Zopir merit life eternal.—Omar, Attend and watch him well.

SCENE VII.

Seid: [Alone.] To sacrifice A poor, defenceless, weak old man!—no matter: How many victims at the altar fall As helpless! yet their blood in grateful streams Rises to heaven: God hath appointed me; Seid hath sworn, and Seid shall perform His sacred promise:—O assist me now, Illustrious spirits, you who have destroyed The tyrants of the earth, O join your rage To mine, O guide this trembling hand, and thou Exterminating angel who defendest The cause of Mahomet, inspire this heart With all thy fierceness!—ha! what do I see?

SCENE VIII.

Zopir, Seid.

Zopir: Seid, thou seemest disturbed; unhappy youth! Why art thou ranked amongst my foes? my heart Feels for thy woes, and trembles at thy danger; Horrors on horrors crowd on every side; My house may be a shelter from the storm. Accept it, thou art welcome, for thy life Is dear to Zopir.

Seid: Gracious heaven! wilt thou Protect me thus? will Zopir guard his foe? What do I hear! O duty, conscience, virtue! O Mahomet, this rives my heart.

Zopir: Perhaps Thou art surprised to find that I can pity An enemy, and wish for Seid's welfare; I am a man like thee; that tie alone Demands at least a sympathetic tear For innocence afflicted: gracious gods, Drive from this earth those base and savage men, Who shed with joy their fellow-creatures' blood.

Seid: O glorious sentiments! and can there be Such virtue in an infidel?

Zopir: Thou knowest But little of that virtue, thus to stand Astonished at it! O mistaken youth, In what a maze of errors art thou lost! Bound by a tyrant's savage laws, thou thinkest Virtue resides in Mussulmans alone; Thy master rules thee with a rod of iron, And shackles thy free soul in shameful bonds; Zopir thou hatest, alas! thou knowest him not: I pardon thee because thou art the slave Of Mahomet; but how canst thou believe A God who teaches hatred, and delights In discord?

Seid: O I never can obey him! I know, and feel I cannot hate thee, Zopir.

Zopir: Alas! the more I talk to him, the more He gains upon me; his ingenuous look, His youth, his candor, all conspire to charm me; How could a follower of this vile impostor Thus win my heart! who gave thee birth? what art thou?

Seid: A wretched orphan; all I have on earth Is a kind master, whom I never yet Have disobeyed; howe'er my love for thee May tempt me to betray him.

Zopir: Knowest thou not Thy parents then?

Seid: His camp was the first object My eyes beheld; his temple is my country; I know no other; and amidst the crowd Of yearly tributes to our holy prophet, None e'er was treated with more tenderness Than Seid was.

Zopir: I love his gratitude: Thy kind return for benefits received Merits my praise:—O why did heaven employ The hand of Mahomet in such an office? He was thy father, and Palmira's, too; Why dost thou sigh? why dost thou tremble thus? Why turn thee from me? sure some dreadful thought Hangs on thy mind.

Seid: It must be so: the times Are full of terror.

Zopir: If thou feelest remorse Thy heart is guiltless; murder is abroad, Let me preserve thy life.

Seid: O gracious heaven! And can I have a thought of taking thine? Palmira! O my oath! O God of vengeance!

Zopir: For the last time remember I entreat thee To follow me; away, thy fate depends Upon this moment.

SCENE IX.

Zopir, Seid, Omar.

Omar: [Entering hastily.] Traitor, Mahomet Expects thee.

Seid: O I know not where or what I am; destruction, ruin and despair On every side await me: whither now Shall wretched Seid fly?

Omar: To him whom God Hath chosen, thy injured king, and master.

Seid: Yes: And there abjure the dreadful oath I made.

SCENE X.

Zopir: [Alone.] The desperate youth is gone—I know not why, But my heart beats for his distress; his looks, His pity, his remorse, his every action Affect me deeply: I must follow him.

SCENE XI.

Zopir, Phanor.

Phanor: This letter, sir, was by an Arab given In secret to me.

Zopir: From Hercides! gods, What do I read? will heaven in tenderest pity At length repay me for a life of sorrows? Hercides begs to see me—he who snatched From this fond bosom my two helpless children; They yet are living, so this paper tells me, Slaves to the tyrant—Seid and Palmira Are orphans both, and know not whence they sprang, Perhaps my children—O delusive hope, Why wilt thou flatter me? it cannot be; Fain would I credit thee, thou sweet deceiver: I fly to meet and to embrace my children; Yes; I will see Hercides: let him come At midnight to me, to this holy altar, Where I so often have invoked the gods, At last, perhaps, propitious to my vows: O ye immortal powers, restore my children, Give back to virtue's paths two generous hearts Corrupted by an impious, vile usurper! If Seid and Palmira are not mine, If such is my hard fate, I will adopt The noble pair, and be their father still.

ACT IV.

SCENE I.

Mahomet, Omar.

Omar: My lord, our secret is discovered; Seid Has told Hercides; we are on the verge Of ruin, yet I know he will obey.

Mahomet: Revealed it, sayest thou?

Omar: Yes: Hercides loves him With tenderness.

Mahomet: Indeed! What said he to it?

Omar: He stood aghast and seemed to pity Zopir.

Mahomet: He's weak, and therefore not to be entrusted; Fools ever will be traitors; but no matter, Let him take heed; a method may be found To rid us of such dangerous witnesses: Say, Omar, have my orders been obeyed?

Omar: They have, my lord.

Mahomet: 'Tis well: remember, Omar, In one important hour or Mahomet Or Zopir is no more; if Zopir dies, The credulous people will adore that God Who thus declared for me, and saved his prophet: Be this our first great object; that once done, Take care of Seid; art thou sure the poison Will do its office?

Omar: Fear it not, my lord.

Mahomet: O we must work in secret, the dark shades Of death must hide our purpose—while we shed Old Zopir's blood, be sure you keep Palmira In deepest ignorance; she must not know The secret of her birth: her bliss and mine Depend upon it; well thou knowest, my triumphs From error's fruitful source incessant flow: The ties of blood, and all their boasted power Are mere delusions: what are nature's bonds? Nothing but habit, the mere force of custom: Palmira knows no duty but obedience To me; I am her lord, her king, her father, Perhaps may add the name of husband to them: Her little heart will beat with proud ambition To captivate her master—but the hour Approaches that must rid me of my foe, The hated Zopir: Seid is prepared— And see, he comes: let us retire.

Omar: Observe His wild demeanor; rage and fierce resentment Possess his soul.

SCENE II.

Mahomet, Omar, Retired to One Side of the Stage; Seidat the Farther End.

Seid: This dreadful duty then Must be fulfilled.

Mahomet: [To Omar.] Let us begone, in search Of other means to make our power secure. [Exit with Omar.]

Seid: [Alone.] I could not answer: one reproachful word From Mahomet sufficed: I stood abashed, But not convinced: if heaven requires it of me, I must obey; but it will cost me dear.

SCENE III.

Seid, Palmira.

Seid: Palmira, art thou here? what fatal cause Hath led thee to this seat of horror?

Palmira: Fear And love directed me to find thee, Seid, To ask thee what dread sacrifice thou meanest To offer here; do heaven and Mahomet Demand it of thee, must it be? O speak.

Seid: Palmira, thou commandest my every thought And every action; all depend on thee: Direct them as thou wilt, inform my soul, And guide my hand: be thou my guardian god, Explain the will of heaven which yet I know not; Why am I chosen to be its instrument Of vengeance? are the prophet's dread commands Irrevocable?

Palmira: Seid, we must yield in silence, Nor dare to question his decrees; he hears Our secret sighs, nor are our sorrows hid From Mahomet's all-seeing eye: to doubt Is profanation of the deity. His God is God alone; he could not else Be thus victorious, thus invincible.

Seid: He must be Seid's God who is Palmira's: Yet cannot my astonished soul conceive A being, tender, merciful, and kind, Commanding murder; then again I think To doubt is guilt: the priest without remorse Destroys the victim: by the voice of heaven I know that Zopir was condemned, I know That Seid was predestined to support The law divine: so Mahomet ordained, And I obey him; fired with holy zeal I go to slay the enemy of God; And yet methinks another deity Draws back my arm, and bids me spare the victim: Religion lost her power when I beheld The wretched Zopir; duty urged in vain Her cruel plea, exhorting me to murder; With joy I listened to the plaintive voice Of soft humanity: but Mahomet— How awful! how majestic! who can bear His wrath? his frowns reproached my shameful weakness; Religion is a dreadful power: alas! Palmira, I am lost in doubts and fears, Discordant passions tear this feeble heart: I must be impious, must desert my faith, Or be a murderer: Seid was not formed For an assassin; but 'tis heaven's command, And I have promised to avenge its cause: The tears of grief and rage united flow, Contending duties raise a storm within, And thou alone, Palmira, must appease it; Fix my uncertain heart, and give it peace: Alas! without this dreadful sacrifice, The tie that binds us is forever broke; This only can secure thee.

Palmira: Am I then The price of blood, of Zopir's blood?

Seid: So heaven And Mahomet decree.

Palmira: Love ne'er was meant To make us cruel, barbarous, and inhuman.

Seid: To Zopir's murderer, and to him alone, Palmira must be given.

Palmira: O hard condition!

Seid: But 'tis the will of Mahomet and heaven.

Palmira: Alas!

Seid: Thou knowest the dreadful curse that waits On disobedience—everlasting pain.

Palmira: If thou must be the instrument of vengeance, If at thy hands the blood which thou hast promised Shall be required—

Seid: What's to be done?

Palmira: I tremble To think of it—yet—

Seid: It must be so then: thou Hast fixed his doom; Palmira has consented.

Palmira: Did I consent?

Seid: Thou didst.

Palmira: Detested thought! What have I said?

Seid: By thee the voice of heaven Speaks its last dread command, and I obey: Yon fatal altar is the chosen seat Of Zopir's worship, there he bends the knee To his false gods; retire, my sweet Palmira.

Palmira: I cannot leave thee.

Seid: Thou must not be witness To such a deed of horror: these, Palmira, Are dreadful moments: fly to yonder grove, Thou wilt be near the prophet there: away.

Palmira: Zopir must die then?

Seid: Yes: this fatal hand Must drag him to the earth, there murder him, And bathe yon ruined altar in his blood.

Palmira: Die by thy hand! I shudder at the thought: But see! he comes; just heaven! [The farther part of the stage opens, and discovers an altar.]

SCENE IV.

Seid, Palmira,on One Side;zopir,standing near the Altar.

Zopir: Ye guardian gods Of Mecca, threatened by an impious sect Of vile impostors, now assert your power, And let your Zopir's prayers, perhaps the last He e'er shall make, be heard! the feeble bonds Of our short peace are broken, and fierce war Vindictive rages; O if ye support The cause of this usurper—

Seid: [Aside to Palmira.] Hear, Palmira, How he blasphemes!

Zopir: May death be Zopir's lot! I wish for naught on earth but to behold, In my last hour, and to embrace my children, To die in their loved arms, if yet they live, If they are here, for something whispers me That I shall see them still.

Palmira: [Aside to Seid.] His children, said he?

Zopir: O I should die with pleasure at the sight: Watch over and protect them, ye kind gods, O let them think like me, but not like me Be wretched!

Seid: See! he prays to his false gods: This is the time to end him. [Draws his sword.]

Palmira: Do not, Seid.

Seid: To serve my God, to please and merit thee, This sword, devoted to the cause of heaven, Is drawn, and shall destroy its deadliest foe: Yon dreary walk invites me to the deed, Methinks the path is bloody, wandering ghosts Glide through the shade, and beckon me away.

Palmira: What sayest thou, Seid?

Seid: Ministers of death, I follow you; conduct me to the altar, And guide my trembling hand!

Palmira: It must not be; 'Tis horrible: O stop, my Seid.

Seid: No: The hour is come, and see! the altar shakes.

Palmira: 'Tis heaven's assent, and we must doubt no more.

Seid: Means it to urge me on, or to restrain? Our prophet will reproach me for this weakness: Palmira!

Palmira: Well!

Seid: Address thyself to heaven: I go to do the deed. [He goes behind the altar where Zopir is retired.]

Palmira: [Alone.]

O dreadful moment! What do I feel within! my blood runs cold: And yet if heaven demands the sacrifice, Am I to judge, to ask, or to complain? Where is the heart that knows itself, that knows Its innocence or guilt? We must obey: But hark! methought I heard the plaintive voice Of death; the deed is done—alas! my Seid.

Seid: [Returns looking wildly around] What voice was that? where am I? where's Palmira? I cannot see Palmira; O she's gone, She's lost forever.

Palmira: Art thou blind to her Who only lives for thee?

Seid: Where are we?

Palmira: Speak, My Seid, is the dreadful sacrifice Performed, and thy sad promise all fulfilled?

Seid: What sayest thou?

Palmira: Zopir? is he dead?

Seid: Who? Zopir?

Palmira: Good heaven, preserve his senses!—come, my Seid, Let us be gone.

Seid: How will these tottering limbs Support me!—I recover—is it you, Palmira?

Palmira: Yes: what hast thou done?

Seid: Obeyed The voice of heaven, seized with this desperate hand His silver hairs, and dragged him to the earth: 'Twas thy command: O God! thou couldst not bid me Commit a crime! trembling and pale a while I stood aghast, then drew this sacred sword, And plunged it in his bosom: what a look Of tenderness and love the poor old man Cast on his murderer! a scene so mournful Ne'er did these eyes behold: my heart retains And will forever keep the sad idea: Would I were dead like him!

Palmira: Let us repair To Mahomet, the prophet will protect us; Here you're in danger; follow me.

Seid: I cannot: Palmira, pity me.

Palmira: What mournful thought Can thus depress thee?

Seid: O if thou hadst seen His tender looks, when from his bleeding side He drew the fatal weapon forth, and cried: "Dear Seid, poor unhappy Seid!" Oh, That voice, those looks, and Zopir at my feet Weltering in blood, are still before my eyes: What have we done?

Palmira: I tremble for thy life: O in the name of all the sacred ties That bind us, fly, and save thyself.

Seid: Away, And leave me: why did thy ill-fated love Command this dreadful sacrifice, Palmira? Without thy cruel order heaven itself Had never been obeyed.

Palmira: Unkind reproach! Couldst thou but know what thy Palmira suffers How wouldst thou pity her!

Seid: What dreadful object Is that before us? [Zopir rises up slowly from behind the altar, and leans upon it.]

Palmira: 'Tis the murdered Zopir; Bloody and pale he drags his mangled limbs Towards us.

Seid: Wilt thou go to him?

Palmira: I must; For pity and remorse distract my soul, And draw me to him.

Zopir: [Comes forward leaning on Palmira.] Gentle maid, support me! [He sits down.] Ungrateful Seid, thou hast slain me; now Thou weepest; alas! too late.

SCENE V.

Zopir, Seid, Palmira, Phanor.

Phanor: O dreadful sight! What's here?

Zopir: I wish I could have seen my friend Hercides—Phanor, art thou there?—behold My murderer. [Points to Seid.]

Phanor: O guilt! accursed deed! Unhappy Seid, look upon—thy father.

Seid: Who?

Palmira: He?

Seid: My father?

Zopir: Gracious heaven!

Phanor: Hercides In his last moments took me in his arms, And weeping cried: "If there be time, O haste Prevent a parricide, and stop the arm Of Seid;" in my breast the tyrant lodged The dreadful secret; now I suffer for it, And die by Mahomet's detested hand: Haste, Phanor, fly; inform the hapless Zopir, That Seid and Palmira are—his children.

Seid: Palmira!

Palmira: Thou my brother?

Zopir: O ye gods! O nature, thou hast not deceived me then, When thou didst plead for them! unhappy Seid, What could have urged thee to so foul a deed?

Seid: [Kneeling.] My gratitude, my duty, my religion, All that mankind hold sacred, urged me on To do the worst of actions:—give me back That fatal weapon.

Palmira: [Laying hold of Seid's arm.] Plunge it in my breast; I was the cause of my dear father's murder; And incest is the price of parricide:

Seid: Strike both: heaven hath not punishment enough For crimes like ours.

Zopir: [Embracing them.] Let me embrace my children: The gods have poured into my cup of sorrow A draught of sweetest happiness: I die, Contented, and resign me to my fate: But you must live, my children; you, my Seid, And you, Palmira, by the sacred name Of nature, by thy dying father's blood, Fast flowing from the wound which thou hast made, Let me entreat you, live; revenge yourselves, Avenge the injured Zopir, but preserve Your gracious lives; the great, the important hour Approaches, that must change the mournful scene: The offended people, ere to-morrow's dawn, Will rise in arms and punish the usurper; My blood will add fresh fuel to their rage; Let us await the issue.

Seid: O I fly To sacrifice the monster, to take vengeance For a dear father's life, or lose my own.

SCENE VI.

Zopir, Seid, Palmira, Omar, Attendants.

Omar: Guards, seize the murderer; Mahomet is come To punish guilt, and execute the laws.

Zopir: What do I hear?

Seid: Did Mahomet command thee To punish Seid?

Palmira: Execrable tyrant! Was not the murder done by thy command?

Omar: 'Twas not commanded.

Seid: Well have I deserved This just reward of my credulity.

Omar: Soldiers, obey.

Palmira: O stop, ye shall not—

Omar: Madam, If Seid's life is dear to you, submit With patience, lest the prophet's anger fall Like thunder on your head; if you obey, Great Mahomet is able to protect you: Guards, lead her to the king.

Palmira: O take me, death, From this sad scene of never-ending woe! [Seid and Palmira are carried off.]

Zopir: [To Phanor.] They're gone, they're lost: O most unhappy father, The wound which Seid gave is not so deep, So painful as this parting.

Phanor: See, my lord, The day appears, and the armed multitudes Press onward to defend the cause of Zopir.

Zopir: Support me, Phanor: yet thy friend may live To punish this vile hypocrite; at least In death may serve my dear—my cruel—children.

ACT V.

SCENE I.

Mahomet, Omar, Guards at a Distance.

Omar: Zopir's approaching death alarms the people, We have endeavored to appease their clamors, And disavowed all knowledge of the deed; To some, we called it the avenging hand Of heaven that favors thus its prophet's cause: With others, we lament his fall, and boast Thy awful justice that will soon avenge it. The crowd attentive listen to thy praise, And all the danger of the storm is o'er; If aught remains of busy faction's rage It is but as the tossing of the waves After the tempest, when the vault of heaven Is placid and serene.

Mahomet: Be it our care To keep it so: where are my valiant bands?

Omar: All ready; Osman in the dead of night By secret paths conducted them to Mecca.

Mahomet: 'Tis strange that men must either be deceived Or forced into obedience: Seid knows not It is a father's blood that he has shed?

Omar: Who could inform him of it? he alone Who knew the secret is no more; Hercides Is gone, and Seid soon shall follow him; For know, he has already drunk the poison; His crime was punished ere it was committed: Even whilst he dragged his father to the altar Death lurked within his veins; he cannot live: Palmira, too, is safe; she may be useful: I've given her hopes of Seid's pardon: that May win her to our cause; she dare not murmur, Besides, her heart is flexible and soft, Formed to obey, to worship Mahomet, And make him soon the happiest of mankind: Trembling and pale, behold! they bring her to thee.

Mahomet: Collect my forces, Omar, and return.

SCENE II.

Mahomet, Palmira, Guards.

Palmira: O heaven! where am I? gracious God!

Mahomet: Palmira, Be not alarmed; already I have fixed Thy fate and Mecca's: know, the great event That fills thy soul with horror is a mystery 'Twixt heaven and me that's not to be revealed: But thou art free, and happy: think no more Of Seid, nor lament him; leave to me The fate of men; be thankful for thy own: Thou knowest that Mahomet hath loved thee long, That I have ever been a father to thee; Perhaps a nobler fate, and fairer title May grace thee still, if thou deservest it; therefore Blot from thy memory the name of Seid, And let thy soul aspire to greater blessings Than it could dare to hope for; let thy heart Be my last noblest victory, and join The conquered world to own me for its master.

Palmira: What joys, what blessings, or what happiness Can I expect from thee, thou vile impostor? Thou bloody savage! This alone was wanting, This cruel insult to complete my woes: Eternal Father, look upon this king, This holy prophet, this all-powerful god Whom I adored: thou monster, to betray Two guiltless hearts into the crying sin Of parricide; thou infamous seducer Of my unguarded youth, how darest thou think, Stained as thou art with my dear father's blood, To gain Palmira's heart? but know, proud tyrant, Thou art not yet invincible: the veil Is off that hid thee, and the hand of vengeance Upraised to scourge thy guilt: dost thou not hear The maddening multitude already armed In the defence of injured innocence? From death's dark shades my murdered father comes To lead them on: O that these feeble hands Could tear thee piece-meal, thee and all thy train! Would I could see them weltering in their blood; See Mecca, and Medina, Asia, all Combined against thee! that the credulous world Would shake off thy vile chains, and thy religion Become the jest and scorn of all mankind To after ages! may that hell, whose threats Thou hast so often denounced 'gainst all who dared To doubt thy false divinity, now open Her fiery gates, and be thy just reward! These are the thanks I owe thee for thy bounties, And these the prayers I made for Mahomet.

Mahomet: I see I am betrayed; but be it so: Whoe'er thou art, learn henceforth to obey; For know, my heart—

SCENE III.

Mahomet, Palmira, Omar, Ali, Attendants.

Omar: The secret is revealed; Hercides told it in his dying moments: The people all enraged have forced the prison: They're up in arms, and bearing on their shoulders The bloody corpse of their unhappy chief, Lament his fate, and cry aloud for vengeance: All is confusion: Seid at their head Excites them to rebellion, and cries out, "I am a parricide;" with rage and grief He seems distracted; with one voice the crowd Unite to curse the prophet and his God: Even those who promised to admit our forces Within the walls of Mecca, have conspired With them to raise their desperate arms against thee; And naught is heard but cries of death and vengeance.

Palmira: Just heaven pursue him, and defend the cause Of innocence!

Mahomet: [To Omar.] Well, what have we to fear?

Omar: Omar, my lord, with your few faithful friends, Despising danger, are prepared to brave The furious storm, and perish at your feet.

Mahomet: Alone I will defend you all; come near: Behold, and say I act like Mahomet.

SCENE IV.

Mahomet, Omar, and His Party One Side, Seid, and the People on the Other Palmirain the Middle.

Seid: Avenge my father, seize the traitor.

Mahomet: People, Born to obey me, listen to your master.

Seid: Hear not the monster; follow me: [He comes forward a little, and then staggers.] O heaven! What sudden darkness spreads o'er my dim eyes? Now strike, my friends—O I am dying.

Mahomet: Ha! Then all is well.

Palmira: My brother, canst thou shed No blood but Zopir's?

Seid: Yes: come on—I cannot; Some god unnerves me. [He faints.]

Mahomet: Hence let every foe Of Mahomet be taught to fear and tremble: Know, ye proud infidels, this hand alone Hath power to crush you all, to me the God Of nature delegates his sovereign power: Acknowledge then his prophet, and his laws, 'Twixt Mahomet and Seid let that God Decide the contest, which of us forever Is guilty, now, this moment let him perish!

Palmira: My brother—Seid—can this monster boast Such power? the people stand astonished at him, And tremble at his voice; and wilt thou yield To Mahomet?

Seid: [Supported by his attendants.] Alas! the hand of heaven Is on me, and the involuntary crime Is too severely punished: O Palmira, In vain was Seid virtuous: O if heaven Chastises thus our errors, what must crimes Like thine expect, detested Mahomet? What cause hast thou to tremble—O I die; Receive me, gracious heaven, and spare Palmira. [Dies.]

Palmira: 'Tis not, ye people, 'tis not angry heaven Pursues my Seid. No: he's poisoned—

Mahomet: [Interrupting her, and addressing himself to the people.] Learn From Seid's fate, ye unbelievers, how To reverence Mahomet whom heaven defends; Nature and death, ye see, have heard my voice, And this pale corpse hath witnessed their obedience; The sword of fate hangs o'er your heads, beware It fall not on you: thus will I reward All impious rebels, all vile infidels, And punish every word and thought against me. If I withhold my rage, and let you live, Remember, traitors, that you owe your beings To my indulgence; hasten to the temple. Prostrate yourselves before the throne of grace, And deprecate the wrath of Mahomet. [The people retire.]

Palmira: O stay, and hear me, people—the barbarian Poisoned my brother—monster, raised by crimes To empire thus, and deified by guilt, Thou murderer of Palmira's hapless race, Complete thy work, and take my wretched life: O my dear brother, let me follow thee! [She seizes her brother's sword and stabs herself.]

Mahomet: Seize, and prevent her—

Palmira: 'Tis too late; I die: And dying hope a God more just than thine Has yet in store a state of happiness For injured innocence: let Mahomet Reign here in peace: this world was made for tyrants. [Dies.]

Mahomet: She's gone; she's lost; the only dear reward I wished to keep of all my crimes: in vain I fought, and conquered; Mahomet is wretched Without Palmira: Conscience, now I feel thee, And feel that thou canst rive the guilty heart. O thou eternal God, whom I have made The instrument of ill, whom I have wronged, Braved, and blasphemed; O thou whom yet I fear, Behold me self-condemned, behold me wretched, Even whilst the world adores me: vain was all My boasted power: I have deceived mankind; But how shall I impose on my own heart? A murdered father, and two guiltless children Must be avenged: come, ye unhappy victims, And end me quickly!—Omar, we must strive To hide this shameful weakness, save my glory, And let me reign o'er a deluded world: For Mahomet depends on fraud alone, And to be worshipped never must be known.

End

CPSIA information can be obtained at www.ICGtesting.com
Printed in the USA
LVOW132305140213

320068LV00002B/530/P

9 781617 202582